Play Lead
In A
Sax
Section

CD 4209

Tenor Sax, Trumpet or Clarinet

MUSIC MINUS ONE 50 Executive Boulevard • Elmsford New York 10523-1325

PRINTED IN CANADA

MMO CD 4209

Music Minus One

Play Lead In A Sax Section
Music Minus One Tenor Sax, Trumpet or Clarinet

Century Plaza

BAND 1
Soprano Sax

BOB WILBER

4096

All Too Soon

BAND 2

DUKE ELLINGTON
Arr. by Bob Wilber

Soprano Sax

4096

Clar. (may be played on Sopr.)
Tenor Solo

The Look of Love

BAND 3

HAL DAVID
BURT BACHARACH
Arr. by Bob Wilber

Clarinet (may be played on Soprano Sax)

4096

In An Old Deserted Ballroom

BAND 4

Clarinet (may be played on Soprano Sax)

BOB WILBER

♩ = 56
1st time Solo, 2nd time Duet with Alto

MMO CD 4209

No More Blues

Clarinet (may be played on Soprano Sax)

ANTONIO CARLOS JOBIM
Arr. by Bob Wilber

MMO CD 4209

MMO CD 4209

A Little Farewell Music

BAND 6

Soprano Sax

BOB WILBER

MMO CD 4209

MMO MUSIC GROUP, INC., 50 Executive Boulevard, Elmsford, NY 10523-1325